PROSPERITY EDUCATION

# WORK IT OUT

## WITH BUSINESS IDIOMS

### WORKBOOK
### B2–C1

**DAVID BOHLKE**

PROSPERITY EDUCATION

Registered offices: Sherlock Close, Cambridge
CB3 0HP, United Kingdom

© Prosperity Education Ltd. 2021

First published 2021

ISBN: 978-1-913825-37-9

This publication is in copyright. Subject to statutory exception and to the provisions of relevant collective licensing agreements, no reproduction of any part may take place without the written permission of Prosperity Education.

The moral rights of the author have been asserted.

Typeset and produced by ORP Cambridge

Cover design by Frill Creative www.frillcreative.com

For further information and resources, visit:
www.prosperityeducation.net

To infinity and beyond.

# Introduction

## Preparing to work it out

Idioms exist in every language. They are common in both written and spoken texts. It's a no-brainer that your English will sound better if you are able to recognise and understand idioms successfully. But in the past, did you have to rack your brains trying to learn idioms? Did they go in one ear and then out the other? Did you use an idiom incorrectly, resulting in having egg on your face?

Learning idioms is no piece of cake, but this resource can help you from the get-go!

### What exactly is an idiom?
An idiom is a group of words whose collective meaning is not apparent from the meaning of its individual words. There is often more than meets the eye because an idiom's meaning is typically figurative, not literal. For example, you know what the individual words mean in the idiom 'hit the nail on the head'. However, you are not physically hitting a nail. Its meaning – to describe exactly what's causing a situation or problem – is not obvious from the words themselves.

### How can I understand idioms?
You may recognise an idiom as you read and listen to English, but recognising an idiom is just half the battle. How do you actually understand its meaning? A good rule of thumb is that, once you recognise an idiom, you should look for context clues.

I hope that this resource proves to be a useful companion to you.

*David Bohlke*

Handouts: pages 3–48

Idiom dictionary: pages 49–73

*Work It Out with Business Idioms*  Handout 1.1

---

F  Martin: Welcome everyone to today's meeting. I hope that you can all see and hear me. As most of you know, my name is Martin Lee. And here with me is Samantha Johnson, our new intern.

B  Paula: Hi Martin and Samantha. Thanks for setting up this meeting. This is Paula Vasquez, here in Barcelona.

H  Lukas: And I'm Lukas Schmidt. I work in the Berlin office, but I'm calling in today from Tokyo. Nice to meet you all!

D  Martin: Thanks, everyone, for making time for today's meeting. So, let's get down to business. I know you all have a lot on your plate these days, so I've only scheduled 30 minutes for this meeting. I assume you've all received today's agenda?

C  Lukas: Um, sorry, but I haven't.

I  Martin: That's fine, Lukas. Basically, I want to discuss our expansion plans into Morocco. Let me quickly get everyone up to speed: Our competitors seem to have money to burn and are planning to expand there as well, so I want to be sure we beat them to the punch. By the way, Samantha, would you mind taking minutes for today's meeting?

E  Samantha: I'd be happy to. I'll share the minutes with the team afterwards.

A  Martin: Great. Thank you, Samantha. The first item on the agenda concerns the timing of our planned expansion. I know you've all been working around the clock to make this happen. Does a spring launch still seem possible?

G  Paula: I don't think spring is going to fly for us here in Spain. I think we'll need until the summer to get everything up and running…

*Work It Out with Business Idioms* — Handout 1.2

|   | Questions | Answers | Which words…? |
|---|---|---|---|
| 1 | After the introductions, who suggests that they start working? | | |
| 2 | Does Martin think that Paula and Lukas have little to do these days? | | |
| 3 | Does Martin quickly get Paula and Lukas all the information they need? | | |
| 4 | Do their competitors probably have more or less money than they need? | | |
| 5 | Does Martin want to achieve something before or after their competitors do? | | |
| 6 | Have Paula and Lukas been working day and night to make the launch happen? | | |
| 7 | Does Paula think that a spring launch is going to work for her? | | |
| 8 | How much time does Paula need for the launch to start operating normally? | | |

*Work It Out with Business Idioms*  Handout 1.3

**Complete Samantha's notes with the words in the box. Two words are extra and are not used.**

| beat | burn | business | clock | fly |
| plate | play | speed | time | up |

## Conference call meeting minutes

Present: Martin, Paula (Barcelona), Lukas (Berlin), Samantha

Objective: to discuss expansion plans into Morocco

Time: 30 mins

Martin got down to (1)_____ right away due to short time available for meeting, and the fact everyone has a lot on their (2)_____

Lukas did not have copy of agenda for some reason (check?)

Martin quickly got everyone up to (3)_____ RE Morocco exp. plans, feels the comp has money to (4)_____ – could easily (5)_____ us to the punch

Timing an issue for some, though they've all been working around the (6)_____

Paula says spring's not going to (7)_____ for the launch – needs till summer to get things (8)_____ and running

No follow-up meeting scheduled at this time

*Work It Out with Business Idioms*  Handout 1.4

**Match the two parts to make questions. Then, ask and answer the questions.**

1. At the moment, do you have a lot on _____?  
2. When was the last time you had to work around _____?  
3. What would you buy if you had some money _____?  
4. If you missed several days of class, who would you ask to get you up _____?  
5. In meetings, what often happens before everyone gets down _____?  
6. Have you ever planned to do or say something, but then someone else beat you to _____?  
7. If your computer broke while you were working from home, who would you call to get it up _____?  
8. What is something that people used to do at work, but which doesn't _____?

a. to business  
b. your plate  
c. the punch  
d. the clock  
e. fly these days  
f. to speed  
g. to burn  
h. and running

*Work It Out with Business Idioms* — Handout 2.1

| | Questions | Answers |
|---|---|---|
| 1 | What are two examples of 'hard skills'? | |
| 2 | What's another name for 'soft skills'? | |
| 3 | What are three examples of soft skills? | |
| 4 | What's one way to identify your soft skills? | |
| 5 | Which types of skills do employers look for? | |
| 6 | What does 'transferable skills' mean? | |

**Circle the meaning (a or b) of each underlined idiom.**

1. A rule of thumb that I try to follow is to pay off my credit card each month.

    a) a principle that is based on experience
    b) a principle that works for you but no one else

2. Writing a first draft of your business plan is half the battle.

    a) the easiest part of a task or job
    b) a significant part of the work that is needed

3. It didn't take me long to learn the ropes at my new job.

    a) to learn how to do a task or job
    b) to learn from past mistakes

4. No one volunteered to organise the party, so I decided to step up to the plate.

    a) to do an easy task before a more difficult one
    b) to take responsibility for doing something difficult or unpopular

5. Our deadline is midnight, so I might need some coffee to push me over the finish line.

    a) to delay a goal until you have more time
    b) to make a final effort towards a goal

6. Kenji is a good candidate for the position, but the bottom line is that we need someone with experience.

    a) the least important fact in a situation
    b) the most important fact in a situation

7. I have only a minute, so can you tell me, in a nutshell, what the meeting was about?

    a) in only a few words
    b) in a funny or interesting way

8. Athens is a great choice for our sales meeting as it ticks all the boxes.

    a) to meet all the requirements
    b) to be in a convenient location

Work It Out with Business Idioms                                                    Handout 2.3

**Complete the questions with words from the box.**
**Two words are extra and are not used.**

| bottom | half | learn | line | nutshell |
| plate | push | ropes | rule | ticks |

1   What do you want to learn, in a _____, from this class?

2   What do you think is _____ the battle of getting a job?

3   What's a _____ of thumb you have learned from your parents or grandparents?

4   What is the best way to learn the _____ at a new job?

5   What country _____ all the boxes for you as a vacation destination? Why?

6   Describe a time when someone helped _____ you over the finish line. What happened?

7   Describe a time when you stepped up to the _____. What was the outcome?

8   Complete this sentence: The _____ line is that the most important soft skill is teamwork. Do you agree or disagree?

*Work It Out with Business Idioms* — Handout 3.1

|   | Questions | Answers | Which words…? |
|---|---|---|---|
| 1 | What do Passive Communicators do when they're asked to help others? | | |
| 2 | Do Passive Communicators tend to suffer the bad effects of a situation? | | |
| 3 | Are Aggressive Communicators open or closed about their feelings and intentions? | | |
| 4 | Do people have a chance to speak when they listen to Aggressive Communicators? | | |
| 5 | Do people hear and remember all that Passive-aggressive Communicators say? | | |
| 6 | Do Passive-aggressive Communicators use humour to make what they say clear? | | |
| 7 | Do Assertive Communicators tend to compromise with others? | | |
| 8 | Do Assertive Communicators help others right away, or after some time has passed? | | |

*Work It Out with Business Idioms* — Handout 3.2

| | Find someone who… | Name | Other information |
|---|---|---|---|
| 1 | gets embarrassed at the drop of a hat | | |
| 2 | is happy to give another student a hand with their homework | | |
| 3 | knows someone who makes it hard for others to get a word in edgeways | | |
| 4 | believes that meeting someone halfway is good business practice | | |
| 5 | feels they have got the short end of the stick at work | | |
| 6 | finds it easy to get their point across during class discussions | | |
| 7 | thinks it's good to put all your cards on the table during negotiations | | |

*Work It Out with Business Idioms*           Handout 3.3

**Take turns to ask the questions (1–9), stating the four possible responses (a–d).**

**Circle the letter (a–d) of your partner's responses.**

1. You have a work deadline. A coworker stops by to chat. What do you do?

    a) Listen so you don't appear rude.
    b) Tell your coworker to leave because you need to work.
    c) Look at your watch and ask your coworker if it's break time again.
    d) Explain that you have a deadline and suggest catching up later.

2. Someone hands in a report two days late. What do you say?

    a) Nothing.
    b) 'This was due two days ago. Get it done sooner next time.'
    c) 'Are you deaf? Didn't you hear me say the due date?'
    d) 'Thank you. Did you have a problem with the deadline?'

3. You need some help from a coworker so that you can finish a spreadsheet. What do you say?

    a) 'This spreadsheet is taking me a long time to finish.'
    b) 'Get your lazy butt over here and help me.'
    c) 'It would be nice if more people were helpful.'
    d) 'Can you please help me with this spreadsheet?'

4. You disagree with your coworker's idea in a meeting. What do you do?

    a) Smile and say nothing because everyone else likes the idea.
    b) Tell your coworker they're wrong if they think the plan will work.
    c) Ask if your coworker is from another planet since the idea is so strange.
    d) Share your concerns in a clear and respectful way.

5. You're planning to have dinner with a friend after work. Your mother calls and asks you to help her fix her sink right away. What do you do?

    a) Tell your friend you need to reschedule, and then go to your mother's.
    b) Tell your mother you have plans and that she should find someone else.
    c) Tell your mother to call your brother, because he's her favourite.
    d) Tell your mother that you have plans, but say you'll stop by after dinner.

6. You overhear a coworker say that he doesn't like working with you because you're lazy. What do you do?

    a) Nothing, because it's embarrassing.
    b) Tell your coworker to say it to your face.
    c) Act even lazier to teach him a lesson.
    d) Ask your coworker if you can talk later about what you heard.

*Work It Out with Business Idioms*                                   Handout 3.3

___

7   Your boss asks for your thoughts on a problematic supplier. What do you say?

   a)  'I'm not sure. What do you think?'
   b)  'They've always been a problem, but that's all we have.'
   c)  'Who chose them? It was probably someone from another department.'
   d)  'I think we should start looking for a new supplier.'

8   Your assistant used double spacing in a report. You asked for single spacing. What do you do?

   a)  Redo the report yourself with double spacing.
   b)  Set up a meeting with your assistant to discuss the problem.
   c)  Ask your assistant, 'Does this look like single spacing?'
   d)  Ask your assistant to redo the report with double spacing.

9   A delivery person brings you the wrong food order. What do you do?

   a)  Just pay for it and eat it.
   b)  Call the restaurant to complain.
   c)  Tell the delivery person they should find a new career.
   d)  Ask the delivery person if they can bring you the correct order.


Number of 'a' responses: ____

Number of 'b' responses: ____

Number of 'c' responses: ____

Number of 'd' responses: ____

**Read the six tips. Underline the eight idioms you find.**

# How to give an elevator pitch

| | |
|---|---|
| 1 | **Say who you are** |
| | This may seem like a no-brainer, but it's important to introduce yourself and say what company you're from and the position you hold. Offer a business card if you have one. Put your best foot forward to make yourself memorable. |
| 2 | **Create interest** |
| | The goal of an elevator pitch is not to overload your audience with details, but to create interest so that they will want to hear more later. You can do this by asking a question, telling a story or sharing a personal experience. Don't let your pitch fall on deaf ears. |
| 3 | **Solve a problem** |
| | Be sure that what you are offering solves a real problem. You want your audience to nod their heads as you speak. If your audience is in the market for something specific, such as a product or service, you will be more likely to keep their attention. |
| 4 | **Let your passion show** |
| | People want to do business with people they like. Smile, make eye contact and let your passion and personality shine through, but don't go overboard. Avoid coming across as fake or insincere. |
| 5 | **Keep it short** |
| | Respect the time of the person you are talking to by keeping your pitch short. Don't beat around the bush. Instead, cut to the chase. Remember, your audience's time is precious. |
| 6 | **Practise, practise, practise!** |
| | It's important to practise your pitch, but you should avoid memorising it. You don't want to sound like a robot. Practise your pitch enough so that you can do it with your eyes closed. Keep things natural and conversational so that you can connect with your audience. |

1 _____ = something that is very obvious

2 _____ = to avoid or delay talking about something

3 _____ = to get directly to the main point

4 _____ = to do something very easily

5 _____ = to be ignored by someone

6 _____ = to do something too much

7 _____ = interested in buying something

8 _____ = to make the best impression possible

*Work It Out with Business Idioms*  Handout 4.2

## Student A

Hello, my name is Jessica Hanson. I'm a sales rep at Better Cable Services. Here's my business card. I'm hoping you can give me just a minute of your time, as I'm sure you must be very busy. Are you satisfied with what you pay for this service each year? Perhaps you're in the market for a new cable TV provider? We help hotels around the country find the most cost-effective cable TV plans. That's where I come in. I won't beat around the bush. I'm passionate about helping hotels save money. On average, we save hotels up to 30% on their annual cable bills. I'd love to talk to you about how we can save you big money!

**Feedback form 1**

| The speaker… | Student B | Student C | Student D |
|---|---|---|---|
| says who they are | [ ] | [ ] | [ ] |
| says which company they work with | [ ] | [ ] | [ ] |
| says the position they hold | [ ] | [ ] | [ ] |
| creates interest in the listener | [ ] | [ ] | [ ] |
| gives the right amount of detail | [ ] | [ ] | [ ] |
| offers a solution to a problem | [ ] | [ ] | [ ] |
| comes across as sincere | [ ] | [ ] | [ ] |
| gets to the point | [ ] | [ ] | [ ] |

**Feedback form 2**

| The speaker… | Student B | Student C | Student D |
|---|---|---|---|
| says who they are | [ ] | [ ] | [ ] |
| says which company they work with | [ ] | [ ] | [ ] |
| says the position they hold | [ ] | [ ] | [ ] |
| creates interest in the listener | [ ] | [ ] | [ ] |
| gives the right amount of detail | [ ] | [ ] | [ ] |
| offers a solution to a problem | [ ] | [ ] | [ ] |
| comes across as sincere | [ ] | [ ] | [ ] |
| gets to the point | [ ] | [ ] | [ ] |

*Work It Out with Business Idioms*  Handout 4.3

## Student B

Good afternoon. I'm Gabriel Mendoza and I'm here representing Pure Life Water Filters. Are you familiar with our products? We have recently completed our expansion into northern Europe and we hope you will consider us for your water-filtering needs. It's a no-brainer that people want fresh, clean water, right? Well, all of our products use high-tech materials that keep water clean and free from pollutants. If you have time, feel free to stop by our booth tomorrow in the conference hall. I'd be happy to demonstrate our product so you can see it first-hand. We'll put our best foot forward, and I am sure you will be pleased. Here is my business card in case you wish to get in touch before then. Thanks for your time.

**Feedback form 1**

| The speaker… | Student A | Student C | Student D |
| --- | --- | --- | --- |
| says who they are | [ ] | [ ] | [ ] |
| says which company they work with | [ ] | [ ] | [ ] |
| says the position they hold | [ ] | [ ] | [ ] |
| creates interest in the listener | [ ] | [ ] | [ ] |
| gives the right amount of detail | [ ] | [ ] | [ ] |
| offers a solution to a problem | [ ] | [ ] | [ ] |
| comes across as sincere | [ ] | [ ] | [ ] |
| gets to the point | [ ] | [ ] | [ ] |

**Feedback form 2**

| The speaker… | Student A | Student C | Student D |
| --- | --- | --- | --- |
| says who they are | [ ] | [ ] | [ ] |
| says which company they work with | [ ] | [ ] | [ ] |
| says the position they hold | [ ] | [ ] | [ ] |
| creates interest in the listener | [ ] | [ ] | [ ] |
| gives the right amount of detail | [ ] | [ ] | [ ] |
| offers a solution to a problem | [ ] | [ ] | [ ] |
| comes across as sincere | [ ] | [ ] | [ ] |
| gets to the point | [ ] | [ ] | [ ] |

### Student C

Excuse me. Did you know that demand for high-end Greek food in the UK has grown by over 50% in the past year? Foodies everywhere are looking for a more authentic dining experience, without going overboard on the bill. That's where I come in. Let me cut to the chase. I plan to open a modern Greek restaurant that elevates everyday Greek dishes to something really special. I'm looking for investors who might back my plans, as I'm sure this type of restaurant will be a success. I think my restaurant could even cater events for your business. It would be nice if we could arrange a time to meet to discuss this in more detail.

**Feedback form 1**

| The speaker… | Student A | Student B | Student D |
|---|---|---|---|
| says who they are | [ ] | [ ] | [ ] |
| says which company they work with | [ ] | [ ] | [ ] |
| says the position they hold | [ ] | [ ] | [ ] |
| creates interest in the listener | [ ] | [ ] | [ ] |
| gives the right amount of detail | [ ] | [ ] | [ ] |
| offers a solution to a problem | [ ] | [ ] | [ ] |
| comes across as sincere | [ ] | [ ] | [ ] |
| gets to the point | [ ] | [ ] | [ ] |

**Feedback form 2**

| The speaker… | Student A | Student B | Student D |
|---|---|---|---|
| says who they are | [ ] | [ ] | [ ] |
| says which company they work with | [ ] | [ ] | [ ] |
| says the position they hold | [ ] | [ ] | [ ] |
| creates interest in the listener | [ ] | [ ] | [ ] |
| gives the right amount of detail | [ ] | [ ] | [ ] |
| offers a solution to a problem | [ ] | [ ] | [ ] |
| comes across as sincere | [ ] | [ ] | [ ] |
| gets to the point | [ ] | [ ] | [ ] |

*Work It Out with Business Idioms*  Handout 4.5

## Student D

Does this sound familiar? You are rushing to get the kids out the door and off to school. You are also hurrying so you can get to work on time. It's a familiar routine – maybe you even do this with your eyes closed. But then one day you realise that you can't find your car keys. You panic. You ask for help in finding them, but your request falls on deaf ears. Well, this has happened to me more than once. In fact, the average person loses their keys several times a year. We can help with this. We've developed an app that helps you find those lost keys – and other items, too! This app is a real time-saver! I'd love to offer you a free trial as we test our beta version. We are hoping to go to market with the final app in six months.

**Feedback form 1**

| The speaker… | Student A | Student B | Student C |
| --- | --- | --- | --- |
| says who they are | [ ] | [ ] | [ ] |
| says which company they work with | [ ] | [ ] | [ ] |
| says the position they hold | [ ] | [ ] | [ ] |
| creates interest in the listener | [ ] | [ ] | [ ] |
| gives the right amount of detail | [ ] | [ ] | [ ] |
| offers a solution to a problem | [ ] | [ ] | [ ] |
| comes across as sincere | [ ] | [ ] | [ ] |
| gets to the point | [ ] | [ ] | [ ] |

**Feedback form 2**

| The speaker… | Student A | Student B | Student C |
| --- | --- | --- | --- |
| says who they are | [ ] | [ ] | [ ] |
| says which company they work with | [ ] | [ ] | [ ] |
| says the position they hold | [ ] | [ ] | [ ] |
| creates interest in the listener | [ ] | [ ] | [ ] |
| gives the right amount of detail | [ ] | [ ] | [ ] |
| offers a solution to a problem | [ ] | [ ] | [ ] |
| comes across as sincere | [ ] | [ ] | [ ] |
| gets to the point | [ ] | [ ] | [ ] |

Work It Out with Business Idioms                                          Handout 5.1

**Read the information on four different teamwork styles. Some information is missing.**
**Ask your partner questions to complete the missing information.**

---

1  **The Contributor**

Contributors are generally dependable, responsible, organised and reliable. When you have them on your team, you don't have to worry about things getting done. That's because they're thorough and task-oriented, and always have their ducks in a row. They are good at **(1)** _____. They care about **(2)** _____. They are quick to provide their team with information and key data. They will pull out all the stops as needed and will use any resources available in a wise way.

**The Contributor**

Question: What _____?

Question: What _____?

---

2  **The Collaborator**

Collaborators are known to be imaginative, forward-looking and goal-oriented, but also flexible.

They are the team members who keep projects things on track. They see the team's mission as the most important thing. They always keep their eye on their prize because they know it's the ultimate goal. Once they set their mind to something, there is no stopping them. They are willing to pitch in and help without being asked. If what the project requires is all hands on deck, they are happy to do their part.

---

3  **The Communicator**

Communicators are seen as considerate, enthusiastic and supportive, but also relaxed in how they approach and take on team tasks. They tend to go with the flow. They ensure that everything goes smoothly **(3)** _____. This may be anything from conflict management to consensus building. Others view the Communicator **(4)** _____. They offer constructive feedback as needed, but in a respectful, helpful and tactful way.

**The Communicator**

Question: How _____?

Question: How _____?

---

4  **The Challenger**

Challengers are often described as direct, outspoken, ethical and honest. They are quick to question why and how things are done. They do not tend to hold their tongue in meetings. They will stick their neck out as required. They are also quick to question the goals and methods, and even the ethics, of the team. This does not mean that they are negative. Rather, they play an important role in keeping things real. They are more willing than others to disagree with the team leader.

*Work It Out with Business Idioms*     Handout 5.2

**Read the information on four different teamwork styles. Some information is missing. Ask your partner questions to complete the missing information.**

---

**1  The Contributor**

Contributors are generally dependable, responsible, organised and reliable. When you have them on your team, you don't have to worry about things getting done. That's because they're thorough and task-oriented, and always have their ducks in a row. They are good at sharing information with their team members. They care about the details. They are quick to provide their team with information and key data. They will pull out all the stops as needed, and will use any resources available in a wise way.

---

**2  The Collaborator**

Collaborators are known to be imaginative, forward-looking and goal-oriented, but also flexible.

They are the team members who keep projects things on track. They see the team's mission as **(1)** _____. They always keep their eye on their prize **(2)** _____. Once they set their mind to something, there is no stopping them. They are willing to pitch in and help without being asked. If what the project requires is all hands on deck, they are happy to do their part.

**The Collaborator**

Question: What _____?

Question: Why _____?

---

**3  The Communicator**

Communicators are seen as considerate, enthusiastic and supportive, but also relaxed in how they approach and take on team tasks. They tend to go with the flow. They ensure that everything goes smoothly by being an active listener and task facilitator. This may be anything from conflict management to consensus building. Others view the Communicator as a 'people person.' They offer constructive feedback as needed, but in a respectful, helpful, and tactful way.

---

**4  The Challenger**

Challengers are often described **(3)** _____. They are quick to question why and how things are done. They do not tend to hold their tongue in meetings. They will stick their neck out as required. They are also quick to question the goals and methods, and even the ethics, of the team. This does not mean that they are negative. Rather, they play an important role in keeping things real. They are more willing than others to **(4)** _____.

**The Challenger**

Question: How _____?

Question: What _____?

*Work It Out with Business Idioms* — Handout 5.3

|   | Questions | Answers | Which words...? |
|---|---|---|---|
| 1 | Are Contributors well-prepared for what is going to happen in their team? | | |
| 2 | Do Contributors tend to quit when things prove to be challenging? | | |
| 3 | Is the ultimate goal for Collaborators to keep their focus on achieving that goal? | | |
| 4 | Do Collaborators tend to give something their complete attention and effort? | | |
| 5 | Do Collaborators sometimes let others do all the work when a project requires everyone's participation? | | |
| 6 | Are Collaborators or Communicators more likely to happily go along with what everyone else is doing? | | |
| 7 | Do Challengers keep their thoughts to themselves during meetings? | | |
| 8 | Are Challengers OK with taking on some risks that others may not? | | |

**Take turns to ask each other these interview-styled questions.**

# What's your teamwork style?

| 1 | What do you do when a team is formed? | a) Find out what others expect of me<br>b) Better understand our basic mission<br>c) Get to know other team members<br>d) Ask questions about methodology |
|---|---|---|
| 2 | What do you tend to do in meetings? | a) Provide data and other information<br>b) Keep everyone in the team focused<br>c) Make sure everyone is involved<br>d) Raise questions about approaches |
| 3 | How would other team members describe you? | a) Factual<br>b) Flexible<br>c) Encouraging<br>d) Direct |
| 4 | What are you like most of the time? | a) Hardworking and responsible<br>b) Committed and flexible<br>c) Enthusiastic and humorous<br>d) Authentic and straightforward |
| 5 | How would you describe yourself critically? | a) A little short-sighted<br>b) Too focused on results<br>c) Overly laid-back<br>d) Somewhat self-righteous |
| 6 | What do you do when your team is in disagreement? | a) Give reasons why one side may be correct<br>b) See it as a basis for changing the team's direction<br>c) Try and break the tension with a joke<br>d) Ask for an open discussion of the issue |
| 7 | What do you believe team problem-solving requires? | a) Having good, solid data<br>b) Cooperating with every member<br>c) Having high-level listening skills<br>d) Asking the tough questions |
| 8 | What do you consider to be the role of the team leader? | a) To make sure problems are resolved efficiently<br>b) To help the team establish long- and short-term goals<br>c) To create a participatory decision-making climate<br>d) To bring out others' ideas and challenge assumptions |
| 9 | What is it about other team members that can annoy you? | a) When they don't complete their tasks on time<br>b) When they don't revisit goals to check progress<br>c) When they don't see the importance of teamwork<br>d) When they don't object to things they disagree with |

*Work It Out with Business Idioms*　　　　　　　　　　　　　　　　　　　　　　　　　　Handout 6.1

---

C　　Caroline: Is everyone here? If so, let's get started. I've set up this meeting today to discuss our third-quarter sales. As you know, sales of our new chocolate bar have dropped by nearly 10% from the second quarter, and we need to do something, and soon. Adam, I don't mean to put you on the spot, but this is your team's account. What has caused sales to decline?

I　　Adam: It's true that sales have indeed dropped 9.5% worldwide, but if we look closely, we can see that sales remain steady in Europe and the Middle East. In the Americas, they've gone through the roof. But sales are way down in Asia.

E　　Keiko: That's interesting. Have you been able to determine why sales have dropped there?

D　　Adam: Yes, I have. It's due to a new chocolate bar that has recently come out of Japan. It's very similar to ours. The company Chico Choco has been advertising it throughout East Asia, and it's taken the region by storm.

H　　Caroline: But why would their chocolate bar cut into our sales?

A　　Adam: Well, although our products are similar, our marketing campaigns are completely different. We have TV and print ads, like Chico Choco does, but they are much stronger in their social media ads than we are.

J　　Keiko: In what way? Don't we also advertise on social media?

G　　Adam: Yes, we do, but our ads aren't really up to scratch, in my opinion. Their campaigns have focused on users creating 30-second videos of themselves dancing happily while they eat their chocolate bar. These are really popular.

B　　Keiko: So, they dance to music?

K　　Adam: Yes, and I think that's why it's been so successful. Chico Choco has its own song that repeats the product name ten times in just 30 seconds.

F　　Caroline: Thank you, Adam. I think you really hit the nail on the head on why they've succeeded. So, we clearly need to step up our game there. We can't copy the dance idea, of course, but we can come up with something creative if we think outside the box. Let's view some of their videos and then rack our brains to see if we can come up with something.

*Work It Out with Business Idioms*  Handout 6.2

|   | Questions | Answers | Which words…? |
|---|-----------|---------|---------------|
| 1 | Who first asks Adam a question that's difficult to answer? | | |
| 2 | Have sales gone up or down in the Americas? | | |
| 3 | Has Chico Choco's new chocolate bar quickly become popular in East Asia? | | |
| 4 | Does Adam think his company's social media ads are good enough? | | |
| 5 | Does Caroline think Adam describes exactly why Chico Choco succeeded? | | |
| 6 | Does Caroline think their company needs to improve its performance? | | |
| 7 | Does Caroline think they should copy Chico Choco's chocolate bar quickly, or think of their own solution in a more creative way? | | |
| 8 | Does Caroline suggest that they think very hard or take a break after viewing some videos? | | |

*Work It Out with Business Idioms*     Handout 6.3

**Complete the questions with words from the box.**

**Two words are extra and are not used.**

| | | | | |
|---|---|---|---|---|
| box | nail | rack | roof | scratch |
| seat | spot | step | storm | work |

1. What's a product whose sales have gone through the _____ this year? Can you explain why?

2. When was the last time you had to _____ your brains to come up with a solution to a problem?

3. Has your boss ever put you on the _____? What were the circumstances?

4. What's an example of a viral video that has taken the online community by _____?

5. What's an example of an item you purchased that you later found was not up to _____? What did you do about it?

6. Do you remember a time when someone in a meeting was asked a question and they really hit the _____ on the head with their response?

7. When was the last time you had to _____ up your game to complete a project or assignment?

8. What are three possible uses for a paper clip, besides being used to hold paper together? Think outside the _____ and come up with creative uses.

*Work It Out with Business Idioms*  Handout 6.4

**Come up with some marketing ideas for a new product.**

Your company produces many types of traditional soft drinks, but, lately, sales of its last three offerings have not exactly gone through the roof. Your latest product is called *Swarm*. It is an all-natural energy drink that, among its ingredients, contains several types of powdered, edible insects. The company feels that this will be its biggest selling point and that the product could take the soft-drinks world by storm. As members of the marketing team, your boss has asked you to rack your brains to come up with some creative ideas for marketing the product.

Use these questions to guide your discussion.

- What group do you think will be the primary market for the product?
- What group could be a secondary market for the product?
- What are the best ways to reach these markets?

Consider these possible marketing strategies, or come up with your own ideas. Then, take notes below on your ideas. Be prepared to share your ideas with the class.

| Influencer marketing | Partner marketing | User-generated marketing |
|---|---|---|
| Cause marketing | Telemarketing | Free sample marketing |
| Event marketing | Direct mail marketing | email marketing |
| Freebie marketing | Tradeshow marketing | Social media marketing |

Notes

*Work It Out with Business Idioms*　　　　　　　　　　　　　　　　　　　　　　Handout 7.1

**Read the text. Then, work together to determine which sentence (a–e) goes into each gap (1–5).**

a) Consider what impact the decision may have when you make your choice.
b) It's useful to write the possible solutions down so you have a record.
c) Write up a detailed plan for implementing the solution.
d) Gather the information you need to define the problem.
e) Consider what you and others need to do to solve each problem.

# How to solve a problem

**1 Identify the details of the problem**

(1)_____ There may be more than meets the eye. Consider the reasons for the problem – workplace rules and procedures, employee roles and responsibilities, and so on. It's a good idea to write down the outcome you want, but don't assume what the solution should be at this point.

**2 Brainstorm solutions**

Think about and discuss every possible solution you can think of. If possible, brainstorm with various people who are affected by the problem so that you can get a larger understanding of what might need to be done. (2)_____ Don't throw cold water on any idea. At this stage in the game, don't worry if the ideas are good or bad.

**3 Evaluate the solutions**

Look at all the possible solutions and evaluate each one. You may feel overwhelmed by all the choices, but this is par for the course. Ask yourself which problems are easy to solve, and which are more difficult. Think about the resources that are available for each one.
(3)_____

**4 Make a decision**

Once you have considered all the possible solutions and narrowed them down, it's time to decide on one solution. This is a piece of cake for some people, but others will struggle to make a firm decision. Be sure that the solution clearly addresses the root cause of the problem.
(4)_____

**5 Take action**

(5)_____ Don't bite off more than you can chew – be sure that your plan is feasible. Get any necessary approvals and then put your plan into action. Finally, cross your fingers and hope your solution solves the problem!

*Work It Out with Business Idioms* — Handout 7.2

|   | Questions | Answers | Which words…? |
|---|---|---|---|
| 1 | When you look at a problem, is there sometimes more to it than what may appear at first? | | |
| 2 | Should you say that an idea is bad during the brainstorming process? | | |
| 3 | Is it normal to feel overwhelmed by a large number of possible solutions? | | |
| 4 | Does everyone find it challenging to decide on a solution? | | |
| 5 | When it's time to take action, is it a good idea to try and do more than you're capable of? | | |
| 6 | Do you implement your plan before or after you get any necessary approvals? | | |
| 7 | Is there something you can do to show that you hope for good luck? | | |

*Work It Out with Business Idioms*  Handout 7.3

**Circle the meaning (a or b) of each underlined idiom.**

1. If something is <u>a piece of cake</u>, it's very _____ to do.

    a) easy
    b) difficult

2. If you don't know something <u>at this stage of the game</u>, you don't know it _____.

    a) at this point in the process
    b) because the rules are unclear

3. When you <u>bite off more than you can chew</u>, you _____.

    a) learn more and more every year
    b) do more than you're capable of

4. You <u>cross your fingers</u> when you want _____ luck.

    a) bad
    b) good

5. If there is <u>more than meets the eye</u>, there is _____.

    a) more than there appears to be at first
    b) more positive than negative information

6. Something that is <u>par for the course</u> is _____.

    a) normal
    b) not normal

7. If you <u>put</u> a plan <u>into action</u>, you _____ it.

    a) start or implement
    b) delay or cancel

8. When you <u>throw cold water on</u> an idea, you are _____ about the idea.

    a) positive
    b) negative

# Building a global brand

If you want to build a global brand, you will need to do more than have a great product and a catchy slogan. You'll need to learn the ins and outs of the culture you are selling into. These four tips may be useful in helping you launch your branch across borders.

1  **Study consumers' behaviour**

   A consumer may have certain purchasing preferences in one culture, but that doesn't mean they are universal. When Walmart built its stores in China, it expected to hit pay dirt. The company built all its stores near industrial parks. It didn't realise that Chinese consumers prefer to shop near home, not near work.

2  **Think broadly**

   A company may one day wish to expand on what it sells, so it's important that a company's name is broad enough. As the company Boston Chicken expanded its offering into products other than poultry, their name no longer cut the mustard. So it changed its name to Boston Market. It was a smart move and the company came up smelling like roses.

3  **Be culturally sensitive**

   It's essential to create culturally appropriate ads that appeal to international customers. The luxury brand Dolce & Gabbana once got into hot water for its ad campaign in China. The ad showed a Chinese woman trying to eat Italian food with chopsticks while a male voice gave her instructions. The Chinese government criticised the ad and sales took a nosedive.

4  **Check any translations**

   A great name in one language may translate into something confusing, embarrassing or even offensive in another. The French cheese brand Kiri had to change its name to Kibi at the eleventh hour when it was getting ready to launch the product in Iran. That's because it realised that 'kiri' in Farsi means 'rotten'. The company definitely would have had egg on its face if it hadn't made the name change!

1 _____ = dropped quickly

2 _____ = got into trouble

3 _____ = appeared foolish

4 _____ = at the latest possible moment

5 _____ = the particular details of a situation

6 _____ = make a lot of money quickly

7 _____ = was adequate enough

8 _____ = emerged from a difficult situation successfully

*Work It Out with Business Idioms*        Handout 8.2

|   | Questions | Answers | Which words…? |
|---|---|---|---|
| 1 | Is it more important to have a general understanding of another culture, or the full details? | | |
| 2 | Did Walmart expect to struggle in China for a while, or make money quickly? | | |
| 3 | When Boston Chicken expanded, was its name a problem? | | |
| 4 | Was the result of Boston Chicken's name change positive or negative? | | |
| 5 | Did Dolce and Gabbana get into trouble for its ad in China? | | |
| 6 | Did Dolce and Gabbana's sales in China go up because of its ad campaign? | | |
| 7 | Did the company Kiri change its name in Iran right away? | | |
| 8 | How would Kiri have appeared if it hadn't made the name change? | | |

Work It Out with Business Idioms

Handout 9.1

---

**K** — Customer: Hello.

**C** — Service agent: Hello. I'm calling from Ace Cable Services. I'm just following up on your recent purchase of our cable TV subscription programme. I wanted to see if you were satisfied with your order.

**I** — Customer: Yes, I'm very pleased. It was installed on time and everything seems to be working fine. They came a little early, but I was home, so that was fine.

**G** — Service agent: I'm pleased to hear that. Here at Ace Cable Services, we pride ourselves on being ahead of the curve in what we offer our most loyal customers. We want to be sure that customers are happy with our products and receive bang for their buck. Would you be willing to take a short online survey for us?

**A** — Customer: Um, sure, as long as the survey doesn't take too long.

**M** — Service agent: Great, thank you. You should receive an email shortly with a link to our survey. Once it's completed, you will receive a coupon for a free movie channel of your choice, no strings attached. Again, thank you for your time. Goodbye.

**E** — Customer: No problem. Goodbye.

**J** — Service agent: Good morning. Genesis Cosmetics. Can I help you?

**D** — Customer: Hi, I'm so glad that I have finally got hold of you. I've been waiting for 30 minutes and I'm almost at the end my rope. I'm calling about some face cream that I recently purchased online from your company. To cut a long story short, the package arrived yesterday, but it has the wrong face cream in it. My purchase order number is 299140.

**N** — Service agent: Let me just pull that information up so I can get to the bottom of this. Yes, I found it. You purchased two jars of the Omega Face Cream?

**H** — Customer: That's correct, but I received two jars of the Matsudo cream.

**B** — Service agent. I'm so sorry, I'll get the ball rolling on that right away and I'll arrange to have your original order sent out today. Feel free to keep the Omega Face Cream. There's no need to return it. Is there anything else I can help you with?

**L** — Customer: No, you've been very helpful. Thank you.

**F** — Service agent. You're welcome. Goodbye, and thank you for being part of the Genesis Cosmetics family.

Work It Out with Business Idioms

Handout 9.2

**Choose the correct answer choice (a or b) for each question.**

1   Which company do you think is <u>ahead of the curve</u> regarding its use of technology?

   a) in need of financial investment
   b) ahead of current thinking or trends

2   Describe a time at work when you felt as if you were <u>at the end of your rope</u>.

   a) having no strength or patience left
   b) being recognised for an achievement

3   What are some ways to <u>get hold of</u> a customer these days?

   a) to manage to contact someone
   b) to help someone in need

4   Have you recently purchased a product that offered you a lot of <u>bang for your buck</u>?

   a) reasons for exchanging an item
   b) good value for money

5   What would you be happy to do for your friends, with <u>no strings attached</u>?

   a) having no conditions or expectations in an agreement
   b) having a good time doing something even if others aren't

6   If someone stole your identity, what would you first try to do to <u>get to the bottom of it</u>?

   a) to find an explanation for something
   b) to accept that you are in a bad position

7   At the beginning of a sales meeting, what's one way to <u>get the ball rolling</u>?

   a) to involve people who are usually not active
   b) to do something that starts an activity

8   <u>To cut a long story short</u>, how did you get your job?

   a) to explain what happened in a few words
   b) to make a story more interesting than it really is

*Work It Out with Business Idioms*  Handout 9.3

**Replace the crossed out words with an idiom from the lesson.**
**Then, write a response to each review.**

★★★★☆

This company is awesome! I'm not someone who usually writes reviews but they are way ~~ahead of current thinking and trends~~ (1)_____ in how they offer ~~good value for money~~ (2)_____. I had one small issue and contacted their Customer Service department. They resolved my problem immediately. I have been a loyal customer for many years and will continue to be one. Thank you, and keep it up!

★★★☆☆

This company has a pretty good loyalty programme. I'm a Silver member and they just made it easier to achieve Gold status this year. They also now send out coupons that you can use anytime, anywhere, ~~having no conditions or expectations in an agreement~~ (3)_____. I had an issue with a recent purchase and they were able to ~~find an explanation for~~ (4)_____ the problem in just two minutes.

★☆☆☆☆

This company seems to have gone downhill in recent months. I had to call Customer Service recently and it took forever for me to ~~manage to contact~~ someone (5)_____. They transferred me to another department and, to ~~explain what happened in a few words~~ (6)_____, they cut me off! I'm at the end my rope and I have no idea what to do now. This company does not care about its customers.

| How to Build Customer Loyalty | | You | Pair | Group |
|---|---|---|---|---|
| 1 | **Be great at what you do**<br><br>A simple way to build customer loyalty is to simply be the best out there. | | | |
| 2 | **Have the right employees**<br><br>Employees who buy into the company's values are more likely to share their excitement with others. | | | |
| 3 | **Know your customers**<br><br>Set up a database with important information about your customers. | | | |
| 4 | **Don't rely too much on technology**<br><br>You may think this makes you ahead of the curve, but customers get frustrated if they can't get hold of a company representative. | | | |
| 5 | **Set up a reward system**<br><br>This is one of the best ways for loyal customers to get bang for their buck. | | | |
| 6 | **Encourage customer reviews**<br><br>Positive reviews will drive others to your business. Negative reviews can help you find ways to improve. | | | |

**Take notes on each text's key ideas.**

| Corporate Social Responsibility (CSR) ||
|---|---|
| Advantages | Disadvantages |
|  |  |
|  |  |
|  |  |

*Work It Out with Business Idioms*　　　　　　　　　　　　　　　　　　　　　　　　Handout 10.2

---

**Read the text. Underline the eight idioms you find and complete the definitions below.**

## Advantages of Corporate Social Responsibility

**Image improvement**

A corporation that is socially responsible improves its reputation among consumers who feel good when they buy from companies that are helping their community. It's a win-win situation. They also tend to trust companies that engage in socially responsible practices more than those that do not.

**Employee satisfaction**

The way a corporation treats its community says a lot about how it treats its employees. Corporations with a strong commitment to social responsibility from the get-go find it easier to find and retain employees. People want to work for companies that care about the well-being of their employees and the wider world.

**Customer loyalty**

As consumers, millennials are a force to be reckoned with these days. They often prefer to do business with corporations with pro-social messages rather than those just out to make a fast buck. In addition, they are more likely to be loyal to one brand if its corporate values are similar to their personal ones.

## Disadvantages of Corporate Social Responsibility

**Increased production costs**

It can cost a corporation an arm and a leg to be socially responsible. These additional expenses can lead to increased prices of its products for consumers. In the end, it's the consumer who pays the price. Many smaller businesses can be strapped for cash so will find it challenging to do both.

**Profits in conflict**

The costs of being socially responsible can be high even for large corporations. Their management teams have a duty to shareholders to maximise profits. This can put them between a rock and a hard place. Managers who focus on social responsibility may be replaced by those who favour profits.

**'Greenwashing'**

'Greenwashing' is term used to describe practices that appear to be environmentally responsible but aren't. Just because a corporation adopts an image of caring for the environment doesn't mean it actually does. While some consumers may react positively to these types of claims, others see them as stretching the truth.

1 _____ = from the very beginning
2 _____ = be very expensive
3 _____ = earn money quickly and easily
4 _____ = have little or no money at the moment
5 _____ = a situation that is good for everyone involved
6 _____ = a person or thing that is strong and powerful
7 _____ = in a situation with two equally bad alternatives
8 _____ = saying something that's not exactly true (to improve a situation)

*Work It Out with Business Idioms* — Handout 10.3

| | Questions | Answers | Which words...? |
|---|---|---|---|
| 1 | Who wins when a corporation improves its reputation as a result of its approach to corporate social responsibility? | | |
| 2 | Do socially responsible corporations find it easier to keep employees if they start their CSR efforts early? | | |
| 3 | Do millennials have much power these days? | | |
| 4 | Do millennials often prefer to do business with corporations that earn money quickly and easily? | | |
| 5 | Does it cost much money for a corporation to be socially responsible? | | |
| 6 | What don't small businesses often have enough of? | | |
| 7 | Do management teams that only focus on increasing profits for shareholders find themselves in a good position? | | |
| 8 | Are corporations that engage in 'greenwashing' being honest? | | |

*Work It Out with Business Idioms*  Handout 10.4

**Ask and answer questions with your partner to complete the information.**

Student A

1 The toy company Lego has reduced the amount of packaging it uses and has started using more sustainable materials in its production processes. It has also invested heavily in _____ [What?].

2 The shoe company TOMS is not all about making a fast buck. Instead, it gives a third of its net profits to charities that support physical and mental health. The company also supports various educational initiatives.

3 Johnson & Johnson has reduced its carbon footprint _____ [How?]. The company also works to provide clean, safe water to many communities. It's win-win situation for all involved.

4 The coffee chain Starbucks has a socially responsible hiring process that aims to diversify its workforce. They hire veterans, refugees, and people who are looking to start their careers.

5 Google is a force to be reckoned with. The tech giant has invested in renewable energy sources. The company also is known for _____ [What?].

6 The streaming giant Netflix offers benefits to support its employees. The company offers 52 weeks of paid time off to new parents. This compares favourably to 18 weeks offered by other tech companies.

7 The outdoor-clothing company Patagonia works with many factories to produce clothes that don't cost an arm and a leg. The company has insisted _____ [For how long?] that its employees receive a wage that is above the minimum wage.

8 The drug company Pfizer focuses on 'corporate citizenship', with initiatives including the spreading of awareness about diseases and provision of health care to women who may be strapped for cash.

Corporate Social Responsibility

© Prosperity Education 2021   39   www.prosperityeducation.net

**Ask and answer questions with your partner to complete the information.**

Student B

**Corporate Social Responsibility**

1 The toy company Lego has reduced the amount of packaging it uses and has started using more sustainable materials in its production processes. It has also invested heavily in alternative energy sources.

2 The shoe company TOMS is not all about making a fast buck. Instead, it gives _____ [How much?] of its net profits to charities that support physical and mental health. The company also supports

3 Johnson & Johnson has reduced its carbon footprint by investing in cleaner energy. The company also works to provide clean, safe water to many communities. It's win-win situation for all involved.

4 The coffee chain Starbucks has a socially responsible hiring process that aims to diversify its workforce. They hire _____ [Who?].

5 Google is a force to be reckoned with. The tech giant has invested in renewable energy sources. The company also is known for standing up against discrimination.

6 The streaming giant Netflix offers benefits to support its employees. The company offers _____ [How many?] weeks of paid time off to new parents. This compares favourably to 18 weeks offered by other tech companies.

7 The outdoor-clothing company Patagonia works with many factories to produce clothes that don't cost an arm and a leg. The company has insisted from the get-go that its employees receive a wage that is above the minimum wage.

8 The drug company Pfizer focuses on '_____' [What?], with initiatives including the spreading of awareness about diseases and provision of health care to women who may be strapped for cash.

*Work It Out with Business Idioms* Handout 11.1

**Write the information alongside the appropriate letter.**

| A | | |
|---|---|---|
| B | | |
| C | | |
| D | | |
| E | | |
| F | | |

*Work It Out with Business Idioms*        Handout 11.2

|   | Questions | Answers | Which words…? |
|---|---|---|---|
| 1 | Do Visionary leaders want people to do just enough, or more than is necessary? | | |
| 2 | Do Visionary leaders expect people to be in agreement on how things should be done? | | |
| 3 | Do Affiliative leaders work extra hard to keep people happy? | | |
| 4 | Are Coaching leaders more interested in people's past or future development? | | |
| 5 | Are Democratic leaders interested in what other people can contribute? | | |
| 6 | What level of quality do Pace-setting leaders expect from others? | | |
| 7 | Do Commanding leaders let others make important decisions? | | |
| 8 | Do Commanding leaders want others to follow the rules they set, or break them? | | |

**Circle the meaning (a or b) of each underlined idiom.**

1. My team is always ready to go the extra mile to make sure our projects succeed.

    a) to do more than what is required
    b) to do less than what is required

2. We can't move forward until everyone is on the same page.

    a) present at a meeting
    b) in agreement on how things should be done

3. The servers bend over backwards to make sure our experience is positive.

    a) to break all the rules
    b) to work extra hard to do something

4. We can't say what will happen to our agreement down the line.

    a) without your input
    b) at a later date

5. I have no idea what Jason can bring to the table.

    a) to contribute something to a group effort
    b) to include everyone in a discussion

6. Be sure to set the bar high if you want to get the most out of your employees.

    a) to establish a high standard of quality
    b) to offer a very large salary

7. Our opinions are valuable, but it's the directors here who call the shots.

    a) to get input from key players
    b) to tell others what to do

8. If you want our boss to like you, I suggest that you toe the line.

    a) to ask questions when you don't understand
    b) to follow the rules without causing trouble

*Work It Out with Business Idioms*     Handout 11.4

|   | Which type of leader are you? | Student 1 | Student 2 | Student 3 | You |
|---|---|---|---|---|---|
| 1 | What's the role of a leader?<br><br>a) To find agreement through participation<br>b) To set high performance standards<br>c) To insist that people do things their way<br>d) To get others to see their vision<br>e) To create emotional bonds<br>f) To develop people for the future | | | | |
| 2 | What's the most important quality in a leader?<br><br>a) Collaborative working style<br>b) Results-oriented<br>c) Authority<br>d) Self-confidence<br>e) Team building<br>f) Self-awareness | | | | |
| 3 | Which of the following best describes your leadership style?<br><br>a) 'What do *you* think?'<br>b) 'Follow my lead.'<br>c) 'Do exactly what I tell you.'<br>d) 'Come with me on a journey.'<br>e) 'People come first.'<br>f) 'Why don't you try this?' | | | | |
| 4 | Which leader do you identify most with?<br><br>a) U.S. President Abraham Lincoln<br>b) SpaceX founder Elon Musk<br>c) Former British prime minister Margaret Thatcher<br>d) Apple founder Steve Jobs<br>e) Talk show host Ellen DeGeneres<br>f) Indian leader Mahatma Gandhi | | | | |

Work It Out with Business Idioms    Handout 12.1

**Complete the interview tips with words from the box.**
**Four words are extra and are not used.**

| air   book   caution   chair   comb   cool |
| ear   hand   man   seat   stone   time |

| Do's | Don'ts |
|---|---|
| Find out about the company and interviewer in advance. Leave no (1)_____ unturned. | Don't send in a CV that contains errors. Go through it with a fine-toothed (5)_____ before sending it in. |
| Dress appropriately for the position. Err on the side of (2)_____ and dress conservatively. | Don't try to take over the interview. Let the interviewer be in the driver's (6)_____. |
| Know the exact time and location of your interview, including how long it takes to get there and who the contact person is. | Don't make negative comments about your previous or current employers. |
| Arrive at least ten minutes before your interview start time. If you have (3)_____ to kill beforehand, use it to relax. | Don't talk the interviewer's (7)_____ off. Sharing long stories or irrelevant information can distract from your qualifications and the overall impression you make. |
| Treat other people you meet while at the company with courtesy and respect. They might be asked about you as part of the hiring process. | Don't exaggerate your experience or qualifications. Never lie or mislead during the interview. |
| Be sure that you understand your interviewer's name and its correct pronunciation. Address your interviewer by title and last name. | Don't be a comedian. Be pleasant, but remember that the interviewing process is formal and serious. |
| Respond to questions clearly. Be thorough in your responses while at the same time being concise in your wording. | Don't ask about salary and benefits unless these are brought up by the employer. |
| | Don't act desperate, as though you would take any job that is offered. |
| Be sure that you understand the hiring process. Don't leave the next steps up in the (4)_____. | Don't exhibit nervousness or frustration. Keep your (8)_____, even when asked difficult or uncomfortable questions. |

*Work It Out with Business Idioms* — Handout 12.2

| | Questions | Answers | Which words...? |
|---|---|---|---|
| 1 | Before an interview, should you do everything you can to find out about the company? | | |
| 2 | Should you take a risk when you dress for an interview? | | |
| 3 | What should you do ten minutes before your interview is scheduled to begin? | | |
| 4 | Is it good to leave things unresolved regarding the next steps in the interview process? | | |
| 5 | Is it necessary to examine your CV very closely before you send it in? | | |
| 6 | Who should be in control of the interview – you or the interviewer? | | |
| 7 | During the interview, should you keep talking and talking to the interviewer? | | |
| 8 | Is it better to be calm, animated, or evasive when the interviewer asks you a difficult question? | | |

*Work It Out with Business Idioms*  Handout 12.3

**You work for a trendy fashion boutique. You are going to interview four people for the position of Social Media Manager. Write five questions you would like to ask a potential hire.**

Student A

| | Interviewer questions | Candidate 1 | Candidate 2 | Candidate 3 | Candidate 4 |
|---|---|---|---|---|---|
| 1 | | | | | |
| 2 | | | | | |
| 3 | | | | | |
| 4 | | | | | |
| 5 | | | | | |

*Work It Out with Business Idioms*  Handout 12.4

**You work for a small regional airline. You are going to interview four people for the position of Flight Attendant. Write five questions you would like to ask a potential hire.**

Student B

| | Interviewer questions | Candidate 1 | Candidate 2 | Candidate 3 | Candidate 4 |
|---|---|---|---|---|---|
| 1 | | | | | |
| 2 | | | | | |
| 3 | | | | | |
| 4 | | | | | |
| 5 | | | | | |

# Idiom dictionary

*Work It Out with Business Idioms*

**A force to be reckoned with** – a person or thing that is strong and powerful

    A. *The new board member is young and seems to lack experience.*
    B. *Don't be fooled by appearances. He's **a force to be reckoned with** in the boardroom.*

A new study explains why women in their 40s, 50s and beyond are considered **a force to be reckoned with** in the workplace.


**A no-brainer** – something that is very obvious

    A. *It was smart to promote Jan from assistant manager to manager.*
    B. *I agree. It was **a no-brainer**.*

Installing solar energy at your place of business is **a no-brainer**. It reduces energy costs and provides long-term price stability.


**A piece of cake** – a very easy task

    A. *I'm worried about tomorrow's job interview.*
    B. *Don't worry. It will be **a piece of cake** for you. You have all the skills they need.*

Any students who have tried to create a bibliography or a reference list know that it's not **a piece of cake**.

**Origin**: The idiom may have originated in the 1870s when cake was often given as a prize for winning a competition.


**A rule of thumb** – a principle that is based on experience

    A. *Should I address people at my new job by their first names, or should I be more formal?*
    B. ***A** good **rule of thumb** is to wait until they invite you to call them by their first names.*

**A** good **rule of thumb** is that you should save at least 10% of your income for retirement.

**Origin**: The idiom is believed to date back to the 1600s when accurate measuring tools were not available in England. A builder's thumb would typically be used to give an approximate measurement.

**A win-win situation** – a situation that is good for everyone involved

- A. *Do you think it's a good idea for our company to adopt a 'flexible hours' programme?*
- B. *Absolutely. It's **a win-win situation** for both employer and employee.*

Hiring students as consultants for start-ups is **a win-win situation**. The start-ups get extra help, and the students get a look behind the scenes at a new company.

**Variation**: a win-win solution; a win-win strategy


**Ahead of the curve** – ahead of current thinking or trends

- A. *Her ideas are very innovative.*
- B. *Yes, she's very much **ahead of the curve**. She may be running the company someday.*

The company's president said that we need to get **ahead of the curve** on our climate challenges in order to remain sustainable and continue to thrive.

**Origin**: The idiom may stem from the shape of a bell curve. If you are ahead of the bell graph's curve, you are staying ahead of everything else.


**All hands on deck** – everyone is needed

- A. *The director wants our team's report by 5pm today.*
- B. *So, it's going be **all hands on deck** for the rest of the day.*

It was **all hands on deck** to restore power in Alabama after Hurricane Zeta hit.

**Origin**: The idiom was originally a naval expression. A ship's captain would call for **all hands** (sailors) **on deck** (a part of a ship) to help during an emergency.


**At the drop of a hat** – immediately and without delay

- A. *Who should I talk to if I need help with this?*
- B. *I'd call Lucy in IT. She can usually come and help **at the drop of a hat**.*

Workers now need to shift roles **at the drop of a hat**, and that requires training in new skills, processes and technology.

**Origin**: The idiom probably dates back to the 19th century, when a man would signal the start of a race or contest by grabbing his hat and thrusting it towards the ground.

**At the eleventh hour** – at the latest possible moment

- A. *Did they submit their proposal in time?*
- B. *Yes, they did it **at the eleventh hour**, just minutes before the deadline.*

The blood cancer survivor who found a donor **at the eleventh hour** is highlighting the importance of stem-cell donations.

**At the end of one's rope** – (US) having no strength or patience left

- A. *I'm worried about Matt. He's been **at the end of his rope** for weeks.*
- B. *I think it may be time for him to look for another job.*

As a single parent, he was **at the end of his rope** trying to keep some normalcy in his young son's life.

**Origin**: The idiom derives from tying a rope around the neck of a domesticated animal, limiting its movement. By doing this, the animal could graze on grass only as far as the rope allowed.

**Variation**: to reach the end of one's rope; at the end of one's tether (UK)

**At this stage of the game** – at this point in the process or situation

- A. *Do you think now is a good time to sell stock?*
- B. ***At this stage of the game** I would have to say no.*

'**At this stage of the game**,' the fire chief said, 'I wouldn't even want to guess what caused the fire.'

**Bang for one's buck** – (US) good value for money

- A. *Which of these speakers do you think I should buy?*
- B. *This one's a little more expensive, but its additional features offer you more **bang for your buck**.*

To no one's surprise, Florida is the US state in which your retirement dollars will get you the most **bang for your buck**.

**Origin**: The idiom has been in use since the 1950s, when the US Army suggested that a stockpile of nuclear weapons (bang) was better value (buck) than a large army. The word 'buck' is a slang word meaning 'dollar.'

**Beat around the bush** – to avoid or delay talking about something

- A. *I really don't how to say this.*
- B. *Don't **beat around the bush**. Just tell me.*

Let's not **beat around the bush**. The country's future looks grim and young people are looking for opportunities overseas.

**Origin**: The idiom comes from a 15th-century hunting practice in which rich hunters hired 'beaters' to drive birds and small animals out of bushes so that the hunters could easily get to them. The beaters would use sticks to beat around the bushes to force the animals out.

**Beat (someone) to the punch** – to achieve something before someone else does

- A. *Did you suggest your slogan idea to your boss in today's meeting?*
- B. *I was planning to, but Sandra raised her hand first and **beat me to the punch**.*

By the time the company announced that it was adding the new technology across its latest lineup of mobile phones, much of its competition had already **beaten them to the punch**.

**Origin**: The idiom comes from the sport of boxing, where the winner beats their opponent by delivering a final punch resulting in a knockout.

**Bend over backwards** – to work extra hard to do something

- A. *There is a lot of competition in the travel industry these days.*
- B. *Many companies are **bending over backwards** to hang on to their existing customers.*

The street vendor wears a Spider-Man suit every day. He's **bending over backwards** to make a sale.

**Between a rock and a hard place** – in a situation with two equally bad alternatives

A. *I'm really unhappy in my job, but I can't afford to quit right now.*
B. *It sounds like you're **between a rock and a hard place**.*

The software company was left with no good options. They were clearly stuck **between a rock and a hard place**.

**Origin**: The idiom comes from ancient Greek mythology. In Homer's *Odyssey*, Odysseus must sail between a monster that lives on cliffs (a rock) and a dangerous whirlpool (a hard place).

**Variation**: stuck between a rock and a hard place; caught between a rock and a hard place


**Bite off more than one can chew** – to do more than one is capable of

A. *I asked for it, but I don't feel I can manage all the additional responsibilities that my boss gave me.*
B. *It seems to me that you may have **bitten off more than you can chew**.*

The government decided to take a leading role in shaping Middle East policy, but they may have **bitten off more than they can chew**.


**Bring (something) to the table** – to contribute something to a group effort

A. *Do you think Omar was a good choice for regional manager?*
B. *I do. He **brings years of experience to the table**.*

Reviewers were quick to criticise the romantic comedy because it didn't **bring anything fresh to table**.


**Call the shots** – to tell others what to do

A. *Do you think Amanda will approve my transfer?*
B. *It's not really up to Amanda. Claire is the one who **calls the shots** around here.*

While the former CEO cannot **call the shots**, he will likely continue to have a large influence on day-to-day activities.

**Origin**: One theory is that the idiom comes from the game of billiards, where a player has to say (call) where the ball will go (the shot). Another theory is that it comes from the game of darts, where the thrower has to call out the exact spot where the dart is expected to land.

**Come up smelling like roses** – to emerge from a difficult situation successfully

- A. *I heard that everyone except Tom lost money in last year's real estate deal.*
- B. *It's true. He **came up smelling like roses** because he refused to sell, and now his investment is worth double what it was.*

Why does the little guy always get hurt, and the big guy **comes up smelling like roses**?

**Variation**: come up/out smelling like a rose/roses/of roses


**Cost (someone) an arm and a leg** – to be very expensive

- A. *Why didn't you join your friends on their vacation to Tahiti?*
- B. *I wanted to, but the trip would have ended up **costing me and arm and a leg**.*

While electric cars can be on the pricy side, recharging them won't **cost you an arm and a leg**.


**Cross your fingers** – to hope for good luck

- A. *Did you submit your proposal?*
- B. *I did. Now I can only **cross my fingers** and hope that it gets accepted.*

With this latest hurricane forecast, let's **cross our fingers** that it doesn't make landfall.

**Origin**: The act of crossing one's fingers goes back 2,000 years. The people in northern Europe at that time would cross their fingers to form a cross, a symbol of good luck.


**Cut the mustard** – to be adequate enough (often used in the negative)

- A. *The temporary employee you sent over this morning just isn't **cutting the mustard**.*
- B. *I'm very sorry to hear that. I'll send over a more experienced temp tomorrow.*

I tried cooking a plant-based burger instead of a beef burger and, frankly, the plant-based burger didn't **cut the mustard**.

### Cut to the chase – to get directly to the main point

A. *What did you do after you greeted your guests?*
B. *We **cut to the chase** and began our negotiation.*

If you're not up to reading the full review, you can **cut to the chase** and go directly to the summary.

**Origin**: The idiom dates back to the silent movie era, when films often ended in chase scenes. A director would sometimes want to get to the more exciting chase scene quickly so as not to bore the audience.

### Do something with one's eyes closed – to do something very easily

A. *Did you do any hiking when you were in Thailand?*
B. *Yes, but with a guide. He knew the route through the forest so well that he could probably **do it with his eyes closed**.*

Isobel set up the product display in record time. It was such a simple task that she could **do it with her eyes closed**.

### Down the line – at a later date

A. *Do you have any plans to go back to graduate school?*
B. *I don't have any immediate plans, but **down the line** – who knows?*

The new auto loans may be problematic for banks **down the line**.

### Err on the side of caution – to be especially careful rather than take a risk

A. *What time do you want to go to the airport?*
B. *Let's **err on the side of caution** and leave soon. The traffic could be bad.*

Due to the flu outbreak, the daycare centre chose to **err on the side of caution** and close down for a week.

### Fall on deaf ears – to be ignored by someone

A. *Did you get a chance to tell the committee about your privacy concerns?*
B. *Yes, but I think what I said largely **fell on deaf ears**. I doubt anything will change.*

The opposition leader's call for post-election protests has **fallen on deaf ears**.

**From the get-go** – (US) from the very beginning

    A. *How is your work on the Miller account coming along?*
    B. *Not great. That account has been a problem **from the get-go**.*

The salon and spa owner said that owning her own business was her goal **from the get-go**.

**Variation**: from the word go (UK)


**Get a word in edgeways** – to have a chance to speak

    A. *Layla completely dominated today's staff meeting.*
    B. *You can say that again! It was impossible for anyone to **get a word in edgeways**.*

Too many virtual meeting attendees means that it's difficult for some participants to **get a word in edgeways**.

**Origin**: The word *edgeways* refers to turning something on its side (or edge) in order to insert it into a small space. The idiom suggests that one must put one's words edgeways in order to squeeze them into a conversation.

**Variation**: get a word in edgewise


**Get down to business** – to start working

    A. *I think everyone is now here, Ms. Walters.*
    B. *Oh, thank you, Dan. All right everyone, let's **get down to business**.*

After taking Monday off, the city council **got down to business**, starting with the approval of several zoning requests.


**Get hold of (someone)** – to manage to contact someone

    A. *Do you know how to **get hold of Marcus**?*
    B. *I don't have his phone number, but here's his email address.*

The bank is trying to **get hold of several hundred clients** who may have had their passwords jeopardised.

**Variation**: get a hold of (someone)

**Get into hot water** – to get into trouble

   A. *I heard that Sofia **got into hot water** yesterday.*
   B. *Yes, she left the office for three hours and didn't tell anyone where she was going.*

The speaker **got into hot water** after portions of her speech were found to be plagiarised.

**Origin**: The reference to 'hot water' dates back to the 16th century. At that time, one way to keep unwelcome guests away was to throw hot water on them!

**Variation**: be in hot water


**Get one's point across** – to make something clear to someone

   A. *I don't think anyone in the meeting understood what I was trying to say.*
   B. *Well, maybe there's a better way to **get your point across**.*

Listening to your classmates' points of view first will enable you to **get your point across** without it seeming too harsh.


**Get (someone) up to speed** – to give someone all the information they need

   A. *Did anything exciting happen in the office while I was away?*
   B. *Let's have lunch today, and I'll **get you up to speed**.*

We'll do our best to **get you up to speed** on the latest Black Friday and Cyber Monday deals.

**Variation**: up to speed; get up to speed; bring (someone) up to speed


**Get the ball rolling** – to do something that starts an activity

   A. *I think we're all here now, Ms. Lopez.*
   B. *Great, thanks Kevin. Why don't I **get the ball rolling** by quickly introducing our team?*

If you can't seem to get a sale, there are several things you can do to **get the ball rolling**.

**Variation**: start the ball rolling; keep the ball rolling

Idiom dictionary

**Get the short end of the stick** – (US) to suffer the bad effects of a situation

    A. *Were you able to close the deal?*
    B. *Yes, but now I worry that we may have **got the short end of the stick**.*

The Northeast, and its coastal towns in particular, may **get the short end of the stick** in terms of weather conditions.

**Variation**: pull the short straw


**Get to the bottom of something** – to find an explanation for something

    A. *Why do you think they rejected our bid? Ours was the most competitive.*
    B. *I have no idea, but I plan to **get to the bottom of it**.*

The reality is that it is very hard for investigators to **get to the bottom of the bullying complaints**.


**Give (someone) a hand** – to give someone assistance

    A. *If you're not busy, can you **give me a hand** with this spreadsheet?*
    B. *Sure, I'd be happy to help as soon as I finish this email.*

Their major concern was that there was a child still in the car, which is why the police asked other agencies to come and **give them a hand**.

**Variation**: lend someone a hand


**Go overboard** – to do something too much

    A. *How many people are you expecting for Kate's retirement party?*
    B. *Only about 20, so I wouldn't **go overboard** on the food.*
The actor is active on social media, but he is careful not to **go overboard** with his posts, like other celebrities do.

**Origin**: The idiom began as a literal nautical phrase during the 17th century. It took on its figurative meaning in the early 20th century.


**Go the extra mile** – to do more than what is required

    A. *This is one of my favourite hotels.*
    B. *Mine too. They always **go the extra mile** to make their guests feel welcome.*

Local rescuer **goes the extra mile** to help dogs with special needs find forever homes.


**Go through (something) with a fine-toothed comb** – to examine something very closely

   A. *Something about these sales projections doesn't feel right.*
   B. *I agree. I think we need to **go through them with a fine-toothed comb**.*

Abigail was advised to **go through the job application with a fine-toothed comb** to see if leadership, initiative or management is required.

**Origin**: The idiom originated in the mid-18th century and comes from the physical action of using a *fine-toothed comb*. These special combs, with their closely spaced teeth, were often used to comb out lice (a very tiny insect) from a person's hair.

**Variation**: go over something with a fine-tooth/toothed comb


**Go through the roof** – to rise to a very high level

   A. *How has your new social media campaign affected sales?*
   B. *I'm still shocked. Sales have **gone through the roof** since we launched.*

With the unseasonably warm weather, sales of garden products and equipment have **gone through the roof**.

**Origin**: The idiom comes from the early 20th century. If something were to literally go through the roof of a house, it would have had to rise very high and quickly.


**Go with the flow** – to do what everyone else is doing

   A. *Do you have any advice on how I could fit in here?*
   B. *I'd suggest just listening a lot and **going with the flow** for a while.*

In this new economy, someone who can **go with the flow** and adapt to fluid situations will be more successful than someone who cannot.


**Half the battle** – a significant part of the work that is needed

   A. *Getting people registered to vote is only **half the battle**.*
   B. *Right. We also need to get them to the polls on Election Day.*

For Australia's animals, avoiding bush fires is only **half the battle**. The hours, days and weeks after a fire bring a whole new set of challenges.

### Have a lot on one's plate – to have many things to do

    A. *Are you free to have lunch with me?*
    B. *Not really, sorry. I **have a lot on my plate** this week.*

Rachael Finch **has a lot on her plate**, but being a mum, model and TV presenter doesn't seem to be enough for the entrepreneur who has also started her very own health and beauty brand.

**Variation**: have enough on one's plate

### Have egg on one's face – to appear foolish

    A. *Allie introduced the CEO to her team, but she mispronounced his name.*
    B. *Oh, no! She must have really **had egg on her face**!*

The senator **had egg on his face** after his lies against his opponent were exposed.

**Origin**: The idiom may derive from the early 20th century, when dissatisfied audience members threw eggs at theatre performers who they were dissatisfied with.

### Have money to burn – to have more money than one needs

    A. *Look at these prices! Why would anyone spend €200 on a candle?*
    B. *I guess this boutique caters to people who **have money to burn**.*

Right now, it looks like investors **have money to burn** as they are willing to buy stocks at nearly double price.

**Variation**: burn through money

### Have one's ducks in a row – to be well-prepared for what is going to happen

    A. *Are you ready for your trip to Dubai?*
    B. *Almost. I'm working to **get all my ducks in a row** before I leave.*

When shopping for a new apartment in a community with a limited number of homes, it's especially important to **have your financial ducks in a row** before the launch of sales.

**Origin**: One theory is that this idiom comes from a popular carnival game in which someone uses an air gun to shoot at plastic or metal ducks in order to win a prize. Another theory is that the idiom comes from nature: a neat line of ducks trails their mother wherever she goes.

**Have time to kill** – to have a period of time with nothing to do

- A. *Where did you get this perfume?*
- B. *I **had time to kill** before my flight, so I checked out the duty-free stores.*

If you **have time to kill** and you want to see Europe, I think going by Interrail would be fun, but it's not an efficient means of transportation.

**Variation**: kill time

**Hit pay dirt** – (US) to make a lot of money quickly

- A. *Did the band struggle for a long time before they became successful?*
- B. *Not at all. They **hit pay dirt** with their very first single.*

JK Rowling **hit pay dirt** with the Harry Potter franchise, and has made millions from publication and licensing deals.

**Origin**: The idiom comes from the 1850s, during the California Gold Rush. In mining, 'pay dirt' refers to the soil that contains a large amount of a particular mineral. When a gold miner hits pay dirt, they have dug deep enough to find enough gold to make a large profit.

**Hit the nail on the head** – to describe exactly what's causing a situation or problem

- A. *Alice says that the reason we failed is because we don't truly understand the end-user.*
- B. *I couldn't agree more. She really **hit the nail on the head** with that one.*

Chris really **hit the nail on the head** by stating that what the firm lacks most is empathy.

**Origin**: The idiom probably has its roots in carpentry. When you hammer a nail, you want to be exact and precise in order to get the desired result.

**Hold one's tongue** – to stop oneself from speaking

   A. *Why didn't you say anything to Julia when you had the chance?*
   B. *I wanted to, but I decided to **hold my tongue** and wait for a better time.*

When Pedro said his friend's business idea was terrible, some said he should have **held his tongue**, while others admired him for expressing his concerns so openly and honestly.

**Variation**: bite one's tongue


**In a nutshell** – in only a few words

   A. *I haven't had a chance to read her business plan yet.*
   B. *Well, **in a nutshell**, she wants a small loan to start a food-truck business.*

The report describes the political party **in a nutshell**: jaw-dropping incompetence and a total disregard for others.


**In one ear and out the other** – forgotten immediately after being heard

   A. *Did he take your advice?*
   B. *I don't think so. It probably just went **in one ear and out the other**.*

It's as if the instructions Kyle received from the legal department went **in one ear and out the other**, and now the project is in serious trouble.


**In the driver's seat** – to be in control of a situation

   A. *Do you think the company will improve under the new CEO?*
   B. *Sure. If she's **in the driver's seat**, I'm confident that things will turn around.*

In housing news, home-sellers **are in the driver's seat** due to high buyer demand.


**In the market for something** – interested in buying something

   A. *I hear that you're **in the market for a new car**. Is that right?*
   B. *Yes. My old one died last week so I've been looking around.*

If you are **in the market for a lake home** right now, you will probably end up paying over the list price.

**Keep one's cool** – to remain calm and not become upset or angry

    A. *Were you nervous during your job interview?*
    B. *Yes! But I tried to **keep my cool** and not let my nervousness show.*

A reporter had a close call when part of a bridge collapsed while she was on location reporting on a massive flood. She **kept her cool**, and, luckily, was able to safely get off the bridge.


**Keep one's eye on the prize** – to keep one's focus on achieving a goal

    A. *I want to be a doctor, but sometimes all this studying gets me down.*
    B. *I'm sure it's tough. Just remember to **keep your eye on the prize**.*

Carol told them to **keep their eyes on the prize** if they want educational reform to be successful.


**Learn the ropes** – to learn how to do a task or job

    A. *Are you ready to take over as team leader?*
    B. *I'd be more comfortable if I had more time to **learn the ropes** first.*

This tool can help new traders to quickly fine-tune their strategies and **learn the ropes** of online trading.

**Origin**: The idiom comes from the world of sailing, where, traditionally, new recruits had to tie knots and move ropes when raising a sail.

**Variation**: know the ropes


**Leave no stone unturned** – to do everything one can to achieve a goal

    A. *Do you think the government is doing enough to find out who leaked the information?*
    B. *I do. They've promised to **leave no stone unturned** in their efforts to find the leak.*

The police department will **leave no stone unturned** in its investigation into the disappearance of the local teen.

**Origin**: The idiom comes from an ancient Greek legend about a general who buried treasure in his tent after a defeat. Those looking for the treasure were advised to turn over *every* stone in their effort to find it.

**Make a fast buck** – (US) to earn money quickly and easily

    A. *I enjoyed the first movie, but the sequel was very disappointing.*
    B. *I think the movie studio was just trying to **make a fast buck** with this one.*

People who want to **make a fast buck** from the misfortune of others are always looking for their next opportunity.

**Variation**: make a quick buck


**Meet (someone) halfway** – to compromise with someone

    A. *Did our overseas partner agree to our latest proposal?*
    B. *Not yet, but we hope we can find a compromise and that they'll **meet us halfway**.*

The new leader hopes to heal the political divisions, but the opposition must **meet him halfway**.


**More than meets the eye** – more than there appears to be at first

    A. *There is something odd about the way Jessica was fired last week.*
    B. *I agree. I think there's definitely **more than meets the eye** there.*

It may not seem like it at first, but a quality yoga mat certainly delivers **more than meets the eye**.

**Variation**: more (to something) than meets the eye


**No strings attached** – having no conditions or expectations on an agreement

    A. *This deal seems too good to be true.*
    B. *I find you should be careful of any offer that claims to have **no strings attached**.*

Corner Bakery is serving anyone who walks through its doors a free cup of coffee, with **no strings attached**.

**Origin**: The idiom comes from the clothing industry, where a flaw in a piece of fabric would be marked by a string. A tailor who wanted cloth without any flaws would ask for fabric 'with no strings attached'.

**Not going to fly** – not going to work well

   A. *If you had the chance, would you like to do your job from home?*
   B. *I would, but the idea is **not going to fly** with my boss and team.*

Whereas the idea of universal basic income might be feasible in some countries, it's simply **not going to fly** in the United States.

**Variation**: won't fly


**On the same page** – in agreement on how things should be done

   A. *We can't move forward until our supplier fixes the problem.*
   B. *I'm glad to hear that we're **on the same page** on this.*

Keeping your remote team **on the same page** as you and your team members is important if you want a happy, healthy team that is efficient and gets results.

**Origin**: One theory is that the idiom comes from singing in a choir, where each singer has to be on the same page of music. Another theory is that it comes from meetings or classes, where each member has to refer to the same page in order to understand what is going on.

**Variation**: singing from the same hymn sheet (UK)


**Par for the course** – normal, not unusual at all

   A. *I heard that we're not getting a raise again this year.*
   B. *I'm not surprised. That's **par for the course** at this point.*

The restaurant is perhaps Tokyo's worst-kept curry secret. Weekend queues are **par for the course.**

**Origin**: The idiom comes from golf, where it refers to the number of shots, also known as 'par', that a golfer needs to finish the entire course.


**Pull out all the stops** – to make every possible effort to achieve something

   A. *I enjoyed Carol's retirement party last night.*
   B. *I did, too. The company really **pulled out all the stops** to make sure it was memorable.*

The singing-competition contestants **pulled out all the stops** for their final performance of the night.

**Origin**: The idiom refers to the knobs (or 'stops') found on a pipe organ that control its loudness. When these stops are pulled out, the instrument achieves its maximum volume.


**Push (someone) over the finish line** – to make a final effort towards a goal

- A. *We want to thank the whole team for the long hours you all put in to this project.*
- B. *It was your hard work and dedication that helped **push us over the finish line**.*

A surprising number of rural votes heled **push the candidate over the finish line.**

**Variation:** push someone over the finishing line


**Put (something) into action** – to implement a plan or idea

- A. *When do you think you'll be ready?*
- B. *I think we'll need another week to **put our plan into action**.*

The company's next step is to **put these ideas into action**.


**Put one's best foot forward** – to make the best possible impression

- A. *Do you feel that you're prepared for your job interview?*
- B. *Yes, I think so. I know I really need to **put my best foot forward** if I want this job.*

All home sellers want to **put their best foot forward**, and that means doing things like touching up paint and mending broken fixtures.


**Put one's cards on the table** – to talk openly about one's feelings and intentions

- A. *Why did you tell her that you were thinking of quitting?*
- B. *I just thought now was the time to **put my cards on the table**.*

The prime minister expressed his hope that, in the next negotiating session, both sides will be prepared to **put their cards on the table** so that the best possible deal can be achieved.

**Origin**: The idiom comes from the card game of poker, where, at the end of each hand, players have to put their cards on the table to prove which is the winning hand.

**Variation**: lay one's cards on the table


**Put (someone) on the spot** – to ask someone a question that's difficult to answer

- A. *Your question about the recent drop in sales surprised me.*
- B. *Sorry, but I really didn't mean to **put you on the spot**.*

The talk show host apologised after it was pointed out that her question had **put her guest on the spot**.


**Rack one's brains** – to think very hard about something

- A. *Did you ever figure out how to solve that problem?*
- B. *I've been **racking my brains** all weekend and I still can't find a solution.*

The young entrepreneur **racked his brains** and came up the idea of selling items made from plastic and other recycled materials.

**Variation**: rack one's brain


**Set one's mind to something** – to give something one's complete attention and effort

- A. *I hope I can come up with a good marketing strategy for our new app.*
- B. *I'm sure you can if you **set your mind to it**.*

Lisa's weight-loss journey taught her that, once **she sets her mind to something**, then nothing is impossible.

**Variation**: set one's mind on something


**Set the bar high** – to establish a high standard of quality

- A. *Sally has just given a fantastic presentation.*
- B. *I know. She really **set the bar high** for the rest of us.*

Sean Connery **set the bar high** with this portrayal of James Bond.

**Origin**: The idiom likely comes from the sport of pole vaulting. The challenge increases the higher the bar over which the athletes must jump is raised.

**Variation**: set the bar low


**Step up one's game** – to improve one's performance or quality of work

- A. *Paulo lost another of his sales accounts.*
- B. *That's not good. He going to have to **step up his game** if he wants to continue working here.*

With only four contestants left in the competition, they all now need to **step up their game**.


**Step up to the plate** – to take responsibility for doing something difficult or unpopular

- A. *Why did you agree to take on that account?*
- B. *I felt like I had no choice. No one else was going to **step up to the plate**.*

World leaders need to **step up to the plate** to find a way to address the climate crisis.

**Origin**: The idiom comes from the American sport of baseball. The batter has to step up to the (home) plate in order to swing at the ball.


**Stick one's neck out** – to expose oneself to some risk

- A. *I'm surprised that my boss didn't defend me more.*
- B. *He isn't really known for **sticking his neck out** unnecessarily.*

While Brenda cares about the people who are close to her, she is not willing to **stick her neck out** for strangers.

**Origin**: The idiom's exact origins are unknown, although some ascribe it to the fact that a chicken will stick out its neck when it's on the chopping block.


**Strapped for cash** – having little or no money at the moment

- A. *Can you lend me €20?*
- B. *Sorry. I would, but I'm a little **strapped for cash** myself right now.*

Consumers are **strapped for cash** this holiday season as more shoppers are looking for the best online deals.

**Variation**: cash-strapped


**Stretch the truth** – to say something that's not exactly true (to make a situation seem better)

- A. *Do you think it's okay if I **stretch the truth** a little on my CV?*
- B. *I know some people who do that, but I think it would be a mistake.*

Some overly eager sales reps may be willing to **stretch the truth** a bit in order to secure a sale.


**Take (something or somewhere) by storm** – to quickly become very popular

- A. *This new game is so addictive. It's **taking the country by storm**.*
- B. *It really is. Everyone I know seems to be playing it.*

The actress's two dogs are **taking the social media world by storm.**


**Take a nosedive** – to drop quickly

- A. *The euro **took a nosedive** overnight.*
- B. *And it looks like it could continue to slide.*

With a massive cold front moving in overnight, temperatures are expected to **take a nosedive**.


**Talk someone's ear off** – to talk to someone nonstop for a long time

- A. *Have you met Les, the new marketing guy?*
- B. *I have. He's a nice guy, but he'll really **talk your ear off** if you let him.*

Ask any local business owner and they'll **talk your ear off** about insane rents, suffocating red tape, burdensome taxes and a shortage of workers.


**The bottom line** – the most important fact in a situation

- A. *Do you have any advice for me?*
- B. *Well, **the bottom line** is to always be closing. That's what sales is all about.*

**The bottom line** is that British higher education is continuing to suffer from the loss of international students.

**Origin**: The idiom initially described the line at the end (bottom) of a financial statement that shows whether a company has made a profit or taken a loss.


**The ins and outs** – the particular details of a situation

- A. *Do you know how to use a scanner?*
- B. *Yes, but I don't really know **the ins and outs** of how they work.*

Not all of them know **the ins and outs** of Korean culture, and if they're not careful they might find themselves in some embarrassing situations.

**Variation**: know the ins and outs; learn the ins and outs


**Think outside the box** – to think in an original or creative way

- A. *Did you like my idea for the ad?*
- B. *You know, I think it's time to **think outside the box** more if we want to appeal to millennials.*

During these difficult times, restaurants need to **think outside the box** if they want to attract customers and retain their business.

**Variation**: think beyond the box


**Throw cold water on something** – to be negative about someone's plan or idea

- A. *What did your boss think of your idea?*
- B. *She listened, but she basically **threw cold water on it**.*

Economists have **thrown cold water on the third-quarter GDP expectations.**

**Variation**: pour cold water on something


**Tick all the boxes** – to meet all the requirements

- A. *Are you going to take the job offer?*
- B. *I am. It **ticks all the boxes**, so I think it's a good fit for me.*

With its array of cool features, consumers are saying that the new Bluetooth speaker **ticks all the boxes**.

**Variation**: check all the boxes

**To cut a long story short** – to explain what happened in a few words

- A. *What happened? Why did the boss call you into her office?*
- B. *Well, **to cut a long story short**, someone filed a complaint against me.*

**To cut a long story short**, the plan succeeded, and the seller received three offers within 72 hours of the day the property was listed.

**Variation**: long story short; to make a long story short

**Toe the line** – to follow the rules without causing trouble

- A. *I heard that you got a warning for leaving work early.*
- B. *Yeah. I think it's best if I just **toe the line** for a while.*

He tells the princess to **toe the line**, to give up on her individualism and accept that the only person that matters is the queen herself.

**Origin**: The idiom originates from an early form of boxing, where a line was drawn on the ground on which opponents had to keep the toes of one foot during their fight.

**Up and running** – operating normally

- A. *Is the new printer **up and running** yet?*
- B. *No, but a technician is working on it now.*

It was announced recently that alternate care sites could be **up and running** within two weeks if needed.

**Up in the air** – undecided or unresolved

- A. *Are you and Miriam going out after work?*
- B. *She might have to work late, so things are a bit **up in the air** at the moment.*

Due to the recent bush fires, Sydney's New Year's Eve firework event remains **up in the air**.

**Up to scratch** – good enough or up to the required standard (often used in the negative)

    A. *Why aren't we having our annual retreat at the Plaza Hotel?*
    B. *They felt that the hotel wasn't **up to scratch**, so they found a better one.*

The best way to make sure that your website is **up to scratch** is to hire a local web designer to help you.

**Variation**: up to snuff


**Work around the clock** – to work all day and all night (to get the job done)

    A. *Has the sales team finished their report?*
    B. *Almost. They've been **working around the clock** to get it done.*

Thousands of customers are without power after the recent freezing weather, but crews are **working around the clock** to restore service.

**Variation**: round the clock

www.ingramcontent.com/pod-product-compliance
Lightning Source LLC
Chambersburg PA
CBHW081920090526
44591CB00015B/2402